M.STEV

Explaining
Mission

Ross Paterson

Sovereign World

Scripture quotations are taken from
The Holy Bible, New International Version.
© Copyright 1973, 1978, 1984 International Bible Society.
Published by Hodder & Stoughton.

ISBN: 1 85240 115 X

SOVEREIGN WORLD LIMITED
P.O. Box 777, Tonbridge, Kent TN11 9XT, England.

Contents

Acknowledgements

There are many to whom I am grateful for their help in writing this book. To my wife Christine, for her considerable help. She is after all a third-generation missionary! To my colleagues in Chinese Church Support Ministries and Derek Prince Ministries – China and Mongolia; to Chris Mungeam, my publisher and close personal friend, who has urged me to finish this book; to Stanley Davies, the General Secretary of the Evangelical Missionary Alliance in the UK, for his encouragement to write from the heart, and for his most helpful comments on the draft manuscript. But most of all to the Lord Jesus, Who has given me the incalculable privilege of serving Him in the harvest field of mission in our world today.

January 1994.

1

Will You Be Lonely in Heaven?

"Those who are wise will shine like the brightness of the heavens, and those who lead many to righteousness, like the stars for ever and ever." (Daniel 12:3)

The Lord Jesus Himself clearly commanded His Church to give itself without reservation to the consuming task of world mission. *"Go,"* He said, *"and make disciples of all nations, baptising them in the Name of the Father and of the Son and of the Holy Spirit, and teaching them to obey everything I have commanded you"* (Matthew 28:19-20). These words, traditionally known as the Great Commission, have often been neglected in the late twentieth century. Today the challenge to reach the peoples of every nation and every tongue with the Good News about Jesus is greater than at any other time in the history of the Church. Yet we find ourselves *less* committed and *less* convinced of the priority of world mission than perhaps we have ever been. We need to return to the words of Jesus and obey them.

If one hundred Christians from around the world today were asked to define the central task of the Church, what answers would they give? I suspect that there would be almost as many answers as there were people giving them!

But Christians in the not-so-distant past had a much greater clarity on this matter. When the heart of God for mission was more clearly recognised some years ago, the students of an Anglican theological college in the UK were so keen to obey the central command of Jesus to world mission that the college principal had to plead with them that some should stay behind, because they were also needed to care for the lost in the UK (which abounded then as they do now). Our values have changed.

7

We have drifted away from God's priorities.

How do we react in our day, with all our advances in modern Christianity, to the following words of David Brainerd, a missionary to the indigenous people of the United States some two hundred years ago? Brainerd died young at around thirty years of age, largely as a result of his unceasing labours[1]. These words were his own epitaph, "I cared not where or how I lived, or what hardships I went through, so that I could but gain souls to Christ... I declare, now I am dying, I would not have spent my life otherwise for the whole world."

I suspect that some reading these words from Brainerd's lips will instinctively feel that he was wrong or unbalanced. They may think he should have been less extreme, or perhaps have embraced other teachings that would have made him more acceptable to mainstream Christianity.

But others reading his words will understand on the level of the heart why he said what he did. While they may not see Brainerd's costly lifestyle as the pattern for every Christian, yet they will be wistful before God, lest they should fall short of His best for their own lives.

If you and I were as totally committed to the task of winning men and women to Christ as he was, our one desire would be to hear the Master say, as surely as David Brainerd has done, "Well done, you good and faithful servant! You obeyed My Word, you played your part that all nations and all peoples might hear of My love."

Oswald J. Smith, founder of the Peoples' Church in Toronto, was a man who put obedience to God's challenge for mission first in his church and in his ministry. He made at least twenty-one missionary tours, through seventy different countries. Smith, in order to challenge his hearers to be involved in mission, used a parable about 'John Chinaman', a name representing those in foreign lands who have come to Christ through the work of Christian missionaries[2].

In this parable John Chinaman was asked what he would do when he got to heaven. He gave a threefold reply. "Firstly," he said, "when I get to heaven, I am going to walk the golden streets until I find the Saviour, and then I will fall down and worship

Him for having saved my soul."

"Secondly," he said, "I will walk the streets of heaven until I find the missionary who came to my country with the Gospel. I will grasp his hand and thank him for his part in my salvation."

"Thirdly, I will search the streets of heaven until I find the men and women who prayed the prayers and gave the money to make it possible for the missionary to come, and I will grasp their hands and thank them for their part in my salvation."

Oswald J. Smith concluded that parable with a challenge, "My friend, will there be any John Chinaman from any country in the world, who will come and thank you when you get to heaven, *or will you be lonely in heaven?* Will no one recognise you except a few of your own relatives and friends? I can think of no greater joy that could come to my heart in heaven than to have multitudes of people (from every nation and race upon earth) stop me every now and again and say to me, 'We are in heaven because you challenged people to pray and to give and to go. You raised missionary money. You came to our country with the gospel. Now we want to thank you for your part in our salvation.' That, my friend, will be a great joy in heaven. Will it be yours? Will anyone ever express his or her appreciation to you for what you did? Will there be anyone from the heathen world who will recognise you? Not if you have done all your Christian work in your own country. Not unless you have invested something in the regions beyond."

Oswald Smith's challenge, while being a parable rather than a theological statement about heaven, must still be faced today. It is an excellent place from which to begin this book. The question we must not ignore is a simple one – *will anyone recognise us in heaven?* Will any be grateful to us because we have obeyed the command of the Lord Jesus, and enabled those who sat in darkness to see a great light – the Light of Jesus?

---

[1]See chapter five for a brief account of Brainerd's life and ministry.
[2]Oswald J. Smith, **'The Challenge of Missions'** (Marshall Pickering).

2

The Mission of The Church
is Missions

*"So from Jerusalem all the way around to Illyricum, I have
fully proclaimed the Gospel of Christ. It has always been my
ambition to preach the Gospel where Christ was not
known..."* (Paul in Romans 15:19-20)

Individuals or organisations which have not defined their
central task will, sooner or later, become redundant. It is the
definition of our task, and our adherence to it, that gives us
identity, direction and energy. This process simplifies the pathway
to success.

Jesus understood clearly His central task and focused on it
without wavering. David Livingstone, the pioneer missionary to
Africa, summed it up this way, "God had an only Son and He
made Him a missionary." The simple fact is that Jesus came to be
a missionary, and everything else was secondary. Every ministry
of the Holy Spirit was manifested in His life. He was apostle and
prophet. He was pastor, teacher and evangelist. He performed
many mighty miracles. He could hold the attention of huge
crowds and yet was equally effective with small groups. He was
as varied in gifting as He was successful in the exercise of it.

But Jesus came to be a missionary. He gave specific definition
of His purpose for coming down to earth in Luke 19:10: *"The Son
of Man came to seek and to save what was lost."* That is why, as
He died on the cross, He could so triumphantly proclaim, *"It is
finished"* (John 19:30). What was it that was finished? He did not
mean His life, because He knew that three days later He would
rise from the dead. Forty days after that, He would ascend into
heaven, where He sits for ever alive, at the right hand of the
Father. Clearly, Jesus knew that His mission to save the lost

11

would be achieved as He died on the cross in our place, bearing the penalty for our sins, opening the way for us to relate to the One Holy God. Jesus had to know what it was He was required to finish if He was to do so. And He did. In the midst of the width and variety of His ministry, there was a central work, so clearly identified, that He could know exactly when it was completed.

Seen in this light, every aspect of Jesus' ministry makes complete sense. From the perspective of such a clear but narrow purpose, Jesus' attitude to Himself and to others is entirely consistent. There is no confusion. Seen outside of this, it makes no sense at all. As Selwyn Hughes has written, "The most successful Man who ever lived, our Lord Jesus Christ, failed by all the human standards that are used to measure success. He possessed no property, left no money, did not write a book, never established a headquarters or compiled a mailing list, and when He was taken by wicked men and crucified, most of His followers deserted Him. All He left were some simple seeds sown in the red furrows of men and women which, energised through the cross and resurrection and watered by the Spirit, have spread throughout the earth and transformed the centuries."

By many definitions of success, Jesus failed. He turned away from opportunities that would have brought "success". He rebuked Peter sternly when he tried to deflect Jesus away from the cross (Matthew 16:23). Yet, Jesus was a total success in His God-given path of coming *'to seek and to save the lost'*. He completed faultlessly His missionary call to the work of redemption and salvation.

This same truth is also clearly evidenced in the life of the apostle Paul, who has such stature in the New Testament. His central task and his obedience to it is totally clear. As with the Saviour, so with His servant. Paul came to be a missionary. He did not waver from that call. On the very day of Paul's conversion, it was made clear that there was a specific calling for Him planned by His Saviour: *"Now get up and go into the city, and you will be told what you must do"* (Acts 9:6). Within three days Ananias is instructed by the Lord to extend the hand of fellowship to Paul and to declare to him God's calling for his life: *"Go! This man is My chosen instrument to carry My Name before the Gentiles and their kings and before the people of Israel. I will show him how much he must suffer for My Name"* (Acts 9:15-16).

Much later in his life, Paul affirmed that he had not deviated from that God-given missionary mandate to go to the Gentiles. In Acts 26:19 he stated before King Agrippa, *"I was not disobedient to the vision from heaven."* Paul received a vision from His Father in heaven which he clearly identified, understood and obeyed.

Jesus, the sinless Saviour, and Paul, the redeemed persecutor of Christians, have in common this clarity of vision and obedience to it. Both knew their missionary task. Both followed in the path of obedience to it. Both could say at the end of their lives that they had fulfilled the call of the Father. They were unashamed workmen. They had given themselves with total dedication to complete what God had told them to do. They were single-minded missionaries.

That clarity of missionary vision and obedience to it is sadly untrue of much of the Christian Church today. Happily, there are some thrilling exceptions – sometimes in lands where the Gospel has only recently penetrated.

As Christians today, we face a barrage of claims for our attention. Each different ministry rushes forward to press its case. Each emphasises its calling in God. But so few Christians seem to be able to embrace the wider calling on the Church made explicit in Acts 1:8: *"You will receive power when the Holy Spirit comes on you; and you will be My witnesses in Jerusalem, and in all Judea and Samaria, and to the ends of the earth."* The clear mandate that Jesus gave to His Church at the moment of His departure to heaven was that we are not only called to go; we are also not to stop going until we reach the ends of the earth. Each new generation of Christians must extend beyond its own limited horizons. Each generation must realise that there is an innate temptation to stay local, and thus to disobey Jesus.

In the Western churches, we have seen two or three generations of Christians give considerable emphasis to the empowering of the Spirit. We have frequently discussed the first half of Acts 1:8, the promise of the power of the Spirit. We have prayed for a deeper experience of Him and longed that we might know His power in our lives. But it is as though we have written a full stop in the middle of the verse. The purpose of the promised power of the Holy Spirit is to reach men and women for Christ. The gift of the Spirit is here unavoidably linked to mission. He is the power Who propels us to go and not to stop until we arrive at *"the ends of the earth"*. A failure to go – a using of that power for lesser ends – is disobedience to God. The Holy Spirit is the Spirit of missions.

If we bring much of the modern Church under the microscope of that second half of Acts 1:8, we are found to be in direct conflict with the will of God. Jesus said that we should go to the ends of the earth, and we are largely uninterested in doing that. Oswald J. Smith said that, "If God wills the evangelisation of the world, and you refuse to support missions, then you are opposed to the will of God." If we are not pre-eminently involved in missions, we are then in direct conflict with the express command and purpose of God.

What is it that keeps us from reaching out, from going in obedience to these commands of the Lord Jesus? Could it be the self-centredness or inward-lookingness of much of the Christian Church today? We are surrounded by Christians who feel that the Church's call is to neglect all else in order to care for them. They clamour that their needs, their hurts and their problems should be the reason for the existence of the Church. They constantly huddle into cosy groups, largely ignoring the cries and needs of the world outside them, many of whose citizens do not even know that Jesus died for them, and are still held in deep bondage to Satan and to sin.

But that is not what Jesus taught. He declared that, *"All authority in heaven and on earth has been given to me. Therefore go and make disciples of all nations, baptising them in the Name of the Father and of the Son and of the Holy Spirit, and teaching them to obey everything I have commanded you. And surely I am with you always, to the very end of the age"* (Matthew 28:18-20). There are great promises here of His presence and His power for all believers. But they are to prepare the Church for its central thrust: *"Therefore go and make disciples of all nations."* The call of the Church is to outreach and to mission. If we stop short of that, we fall short of the call and command of God.

Nor are some emphases in modern churches consistent with Paul's life and teaching. In 2 Corinthians 5:14 he clearly reveals his inner motivation for mission: *"For Christ's love compels us, because we are convinced that One died for all..."* Paul had experienced in His own life the redeeming love of Jesus. He knew that without that love he would have been lost for eternity, separated from God. He was acutely aware that he owed everything to the love of God manifested in Christ's death on the cross. All that he had came from the grace and mercy of God. And that love became a surging power within Paul, driving him on, that others might have an opportunity to taste and see the goodness of his Lord and Master. He was passionately in love with Jesus, and that love compelled him outwards, to the ends of the earth, to share his great secret with others.

Our spiritual sophistication can sometimes keep us from comparing ourselves with Paul. Does the love of God constrain us with powerful urgings to reach others for Christ? Can we honestly say that, like Paul, we are moved by such deep passions from the heart of God?

The Scriptures encourage us to evaluate ourselves in the light of this central command of Jesus. We are to be a 'going' Church, constantly thrusting outwards from our warm communities to bring the light and the love of Jesus to others. If, as David Livingstone said, God made His only Son into a missionary, then we must follow His example as churches today. We must be marked out as a 'going' and not a retreating people. We must be those who surrender the best of our sons and daughters to world mission and not just to local concerns.

Peter Lewis has said that world mission, far from being the main work of today's Church, is in fact "the Church's withered arm". He rightly states that a call to world mission is at the heart of Christianity – "of our faith, our missionary God, our Bible, the Holy Spirit, our Saviour Himself. Mission is not an activity of the Church but is an attribute of God. It is God's activity in which He includes the Church. The Church is thus caught up in a missionary movement for God. It is caught in His flow." The simple fact is that, "There is Church because there is mission, not mission because there is Church."

There is a Church because there is mission. Any other call, any other claimant for the final attention of the Church is a usurper. All others are servants of the task, not masters of it. To set ourselves to obey God again in this matter will take more than information and knowledge. It will take all that we have and all that we are, the kind of obedience that Jesus showed and that Paul showed. All heaven waits for that in expectation. And all the forces of hell wait for it – in trepidation.

3

Defining
The Task

"How, then, can they call on the One they have not believed in? And how can they believe in the One of Whom they have not heard? And how can they hear without someone preaching to them?" (Romans 10:14)

Oswald J. Smith observed that "the supreme task of the Church is the evangelisation of the world." Once we agree with that, we must make sure that we understand what that supreme task involves.

The missionary task can be reduced to two fundamental and complementary elements. The first element is that every man, woman and child should hear, understand and have opportunity to respond to the Gospel. The second element is that every man, woman and child should have access to the Scriptures and to a worshipping and witnessing church, preferably in their own language. The challenge is as simple – and as all-embracing – as that.

We easily forget that all of us owe so much to those who in the past obeyed the Lord's command and became missionaries. Logically, wherever the Church exists today, it is only because at some time or another someone became a missionary and brought the Gospel there. Whether we appreciate it or not, in many of our homelands a very high price was paid to bring us the Gospel that we now enjoy and so easily take for granted.

But our debt to the principles of mission is even more basic than that. Every one of us was once a "mission field". The people who led us to Christ were "missionaries". They came and they loved us. The ways in which that happened were varied. But the heart of the matter is the same – we had the opportunity to hear that Jesus died for us, in a language that we understood. We responded, received Him as Saviour, and were born again. Then our 'missionary' friends helped us to find a church in which we could hear God's Word, worship Him and pray to Him, once more in a language and in ways that helped rather than hindered us to get to know the Saviour better. That, in microcosm, is what mission is all about. The only difference is the scale of the challenge. We are called to reach billions of people in thousands of different cultures and languages.

In this chapter we need to look at these two fundamental elements of mission in more detail. *The first fundamental element is the requirement that every man, woman and child should hear, understand and have opportunity to respond to the Gospel.*

Jesus made it very clear that this was vitally necessary. Addressing His disciples, He said, *"I am the way and the truth and the life. No one comes to the Father except through Me"* (John 14:6). He was adamant that there was no way of salvation in any other religion or any other name. Those who argue that that is an arrogant position must face the fact that Jesus Himself was the One Who made that claim. It is not the unreal view of bigoted Christians.

The early Church also believed that Jesus was totally unique. *"Salvation is found in no one else, for there is no other name under heaven given to men by which we must be saved"* (Acts 4:12). Peter, John, Paul and many others went out, and in many cases faced death by martyrdom under the clear conviction that only by faith in Jesus could men and women find eternal life. Any other 'name' or 'way' resulted only in eternal separation from God. That was the driving force behind those early Christians who covered vast tracts of the then known world, seeking to enable folk to know the choice that they faced, one which would decide their eternal destiny.

Each generation must face this challenge anew. What is past is gone. The future has not yet come. The present is our responsibility. Therefore, each of us must accept this charge to share the Gospel with those alive in our world today. Nobody else can help us. There will be no second chance, no cosmic re-run.

Today, we still have a long way to go. A few years ago it was claimed that 2,236,000,000 people – more than two fifths of the world's population – have yet to hear the Good News about Jesus explained in a way that they can understand. They must hear in their own language, and in a cultural setting that will help, not hinder them, to embrace Jesus. This challenges us to break free from our isolated church ghettos, from which we claim to serve God.

The same source reports that four out of every five Protestant churches in the UK have no one directly involved in overseas mission. What flagrant disobedience this is to God's charge to take the Gospel into all the world. There are more people selling Avon in the USA than there are missionaries in the whole world. Is money really a more powerful motivator than the promise of heaven and the threat of hell for each one of the people in our world at this time?

Even when we do obey, the facts and figures are not encouraging. Only one out of every 171 full-time mission workers is active in cultures where the Gospel has yet to penetrate. Only one in ten of the world's population speaks English as their first language. But nine out of ten ordained preachers are ministering to that one in ten who speak English. Will the other nine ever hear in their own language?

Christians today must live with a powerful sense of burden for the eternal state of all men and women. It is the call of Christ to His Church. That means that our prayers, finances and manpower are to be given without restraint to enable all the people of our world to have the opportunity to hear of the saving love of Jesus. They have no other hope for eternity. If we are to obey the call of God to help every man, woman and child to hear, understand and have opportunity to respond to the Gospel, then there are going to have to be dramatic changes in our values and actions as Christians.

*The **second fundamental element** of world evangelisation is that every man, woman and child should have access to the Scriptures and to a worshipping and witnessing church, preferably in their own language.* Simply defined, that means that when new Christians want to follow Christ after receiving Him as

Saviour, they should have access to churches that teach the Bible and worship God in their own language, and in cultural forms which, whilst being thoroughly consistent with the Bible, do not give unnecessary offence. This involves the planting and establishing of indigenous churches for each group that does not have them.

This second task is as demanding as the first one. One in four people groups in the world today still does not have a viable church. 3,600 languages still have no translated portion of the Bible. While the library of an average church minister in the UK contains fifty feet of Christian books, an African church pastor has on average only one foot of books. Many church leaders in China, with hundreds of new believers to nurture, have no Bibles or Christian books of any kind to help them.

The preaching of the Gospel to every man, women and child and the birthing amongst them of indigenous churches are thus the two great challenges we face. Everything that we do and say should serve these two great aims. Yet the average British Protestant adult gives less than twenty pence (or thirty US cents) a week to support world mission. We have a long way to go. We value the souls of our fellow human beings less than the price of one daily newspaper.

Previous generations were clearer than we are on the urgency of this task. John Wesley said to the early Methodists that, "You have one business on earth – to save souls." Oswald Smith brought that into sharp focus with this challenge, "Why should anyone hear the Gospel twice before everyone has heard it once?" J. L. Ewen articulated a basic personal philosophy, "As long as there are millions destitute of the Word of God and the knowledge of Jesus Christ, it will be impossible for me to devote my time and energy to those who have both."

The definition of world mission, of the supreme task of the Church, is no more complicated than that. It is not in dispute. The only matter still to be settled is whether we, as Christians and as churches, will embrace it.

4

Dark Myths and
Devilish Strategies

"We believed missionaries to be somewhat of an oddity, a throwback of Church history... Missionaries were religious kamikazes ... We admired their dedication to the Kingdom of God, but questioned their sanity!" Comment from a Western Christian – before he became a missionary himself!

The current indifference of many Christians to the task of reaching the ends of the world with the Good News of Jesus is not easy to understand. It is in total contradiction to biblical Christianity and to classic Christian values. How could it have happened?

It is hard to avoid the conclusion that we have somehow been deceived by the devil. Satan knows the Scriptures, whether we do or not. He is only too aware of the promise of Matthew 24:14, *"And this Gospel of the Kingdom will be preached in the whole world as a testimony to all nations, and then the end will come."* This verse clearly states that if we as Christians commit ourselves to testifying about the Lord Jesus in all nations, we will be implementing the programme that leads to His return. The devil knows that – and is terrified that one day we too might tumble to it. If he can stop us working towards that promise, he might delay these events. It is a matter of basic logic. It is in Satan's most fundamental interest, knowing that Jesus will cast him into the fires of hell on His return, to use every tactic to deceive us and thus delay the second coming of the Saviour. His need to prevent the Church from preaching the Gospel of the Kingdom in the whole world is as clear as it is desperate.

As he considers the Church, the devil sees how it is growing. He sees the astonishing growth in South Korea, China and in other lands where churches which were so small at the beginning of this century now are experiencing unparalleled growth. He also sees how these new churches are aggressive in missionary outreach. He is aware that the Spirit of God is moving in power in certain African and South American countries, and of new possibilities for the Gospel in lands like Albania and Mongolia.

He knows his time is short. If these models are repeated, then other currently unreached nations will be invaded by the Gospel and by the Spirit of God. He must act quickly. He must keep in its deep sleep that section of the Church which is slumbering. He must also inflict a similar sleep of deception on the churches that are awake and active.

The kingdom of darkness is therefore engaged in implementing an unrelenting and focused strategy. Its major aim is to hinder Christians from obeying the command of the Lord Jesus to reach the ends of the earth with the Gospel. That strategy contains at least four elements, designed to prevent the return of Jesus for many millennia, were that possible. It is also designed to deliver millions of human beings to hell, a place originally reserved for Satan himself.

There must be a counter-attack by the Church of Jesus Christ, the whole of that Church, to this satanic onslaught of deception. Thus both the four elements of the strategy and our required responses are listed below.

*The **first** element is to persuade us that mission is the task of a small section of the Church, not the task of the whole Body of Christ.* At first, the devil does not discredit mission, but simply relegates it in our minds to a position of minor importance. He persuades us that mission, though legitimate, is the responsibility of a very limited number of Christians, a specialised task force. Church leaders under this influence begin to believe that mission is not their responsibility before God. They therefore delegate it to subcommittees – who are sometimes powerless to change or effect much in the churches. Thus it is easy for the devil to exile mission to obscurity, whilst the prayer, money and energy of the Church is diverted to other less strategic needs. The Church begins to see missionaries as it sees brain surgeons – they are needed in the world, but are hopefully never to be encountered in normal life. They are seen as more and more irrelevant to the regular life of the Church.

It is only as we understand the depths of this satanic strategy that we will be able to defeat it. The sadness of any deception of Satan is that we take the deception as truth, and in so doing deny the Word of God. It is totally indisputable from the New Testament that the whole Church (not just a part of it) should be involved in mission. The satanic strategy will only be countered when we recognise and embrace that truth.

We have to banish the idea that churches are capable of obeying God's command to involvement in mission solely through mission committees. Every church has to be mission-orientated, beginning with its pastors and elders. Church leaders have to be ready to go themselves, and to be sent themselves. They have to live and eat and breathe mission. They have to take their place on mission committees. Ideally, the eldership itself will take over from the mission committee. Most Christians are not stupid. If they perceive that their leadership does not believe in something, they do not do it. That is how it is with mission.

Secondly, when the devil has relegated mission to a place of obscurity, he then depicts missionaries as "odd-balls". Some modern Christians are easily persuaded that missionaries are out of step with the 'real Church'. Missionaries begin to seem more and more irrelevant. Because they are away for long periods, obeying the Master and going to the ends of the earth, they are seen as less and less in touch with local trends. They are seen as obscure people in pith-helmets, their clothing out of date. They do not know the latest songs, but rather talk of unheard of places and peoples which are far from the understanding of mainstream Christianity. Thus, most Christians look upon them as nice, but irrelevant and ill-informed.

A letter containing the quotation at the top of this chapter was written by a missionary who was on his way to Africa. He was reflecting on attitudes he once held to missionaries – before becoming one himself. "The biggest surprise in all of this," he wrote, "is what He (Jesus Christ) has quietly revealed to us about ourselves, our attitudes, and our perception of 'missionary types'. We believed them to be something of an oddity, a throwback of

Church history who were certainly more spiritual than other people. Missionaries were religious kamikazes, determined to crash themselves into the powers of darkness in some remote and irrelevant God-forsaken jungle. We admired their dedication to the Kingdom of God, but questioned their sanity! After all, what people in their right minds would want to move from the familiar comforts of their own culture, to risk health, financial potential and even possibly their lives, to minister to strange and perhaps dangerous heathen? Like many others with a call to full-time service, we would dodge the thought that God might send us to any far away place. Fear – the enemy we all seem to have to face!"

We must once again study together the Scriptures on the subject of mission and read the classic missionary books about Hudson Taylor, David Brainerd, John Wesley, Amy Carmichael and others like them. We need to see these great truths in the biographies and other books that have been written over the centuries, including some wonderful modern examples. We have to see again that if God's only Son was a missionary, and the apostle Paul, the most significant man in the New Testament apart from Christ, was a missionary, then far from being "religious kamikazes", "missionary-types" are at the heart of New Testament Christianity. They are neither so spiritual as to be out of our reach, nor so odd as to be avoided at all costs. They are ordinary people who have set out simply to do what God tells us all to do.

Thirdly, the devil wants to persuade Christians to drift away from submission to the authority of the Bible. The truth of God's word is the enemy of all that the forces of darkness stand for. It is also the source of passion for mission, for it shows us the heart of God. As the Holy Spirit comes upon God's Word and upon us with power, we move out with God's love for a lost world. Thus the enemy must at all costs stop the followers of Jesus from believing, and especially from obeying, the Bible.

A central element of this task of Satan is to convince Christians that Jesus is not the only way of salvation, and that the followers of all religions will be saved as long as they are sincere. Christians who believe that lie will cease to believe that the

Gospel of Jesus Christ is the only message of hope for time and for eternity. When that happens, they will also cease to be willing to pay any kind of price for Jesus. They stop going to the ends of the earth with the Gospel.

At the end of 1993, Richard Ostling, the Religious Editor of *"Time"* Magazine, covered the ten stories he expected to be the most significant between then and the year 2000. One projected story is the continuing drift of America away from the Bible. Another is the decrease in support for world missions. Ostling believes that more and more people will question the validity of efforts to try to convert adherents of other religions to Christianity. But, in contrast to the previous two, Ostling suggested that there will be a resurgence of Islam. This will be the big religious story of the Nineties. By the end of the decade, Ostling said, there will probably be more Moslems than Jews in the US. The irony of these projections is that some Western Christians will be less and less committed to Christ and to the Scriptures at a time when they most need to be so.

It is indeed time to stand on God's word – to live and to die by it. We have to recommit ourselves to the authority of the Bible, the Word of God, on mission and every matter. That will take a determination to swim against the tide. It will include frequent teaching on mission from the pulpit. We need more than occasional missionary weekends. We must have *regular* biblical teaching on mission. Christians need to submit again to the fact that Jesus is the only way of salvation, and that we are called to go His costly way to bring that Good News to others.

Fourthly, the devil seeks to persuade us that our main concern should be with our own personal needs. We begin to concentrate on our own hurts and pains – of which the devil may supply an unlimited number. In such a climate we will begin to revel in the subjective experiences of Christianity – those ministries that make us feel good and seem to bless us. We are persuaded to seek after any ministry that brings us physical or emotional comfort, and to avoid any ministry that challenges us to go the way of the cross of Christ.

At the same time, the New Testament models begin to be rubbished. For example, Paul is caricatured as a male chauvinist, a child of his cultural times. These genuine models are replaced by a twentieth century model which paints 'me' as the centre of creation, 'my needs' as the focus of all attention, and 'my ministry' as the most important. God's authority revealed in the Bible is removed and replaced with the collected thoughts of some modern Christian – or non-Christian – thinkers.

As Christians thus concentrate on themselves, they forget mission and the missionaries. They do not pray for them, and so risk God's protection being removed from those who are on the front line of battle. Christians at home no longer care for the families of those involved in mission or for their personal needs. The missionaries are therefore discouraged in the battle, as home churches forget to write to them, and to care for them in practical ways.

It is time to believe the truth that it is more blessed to give than to receive. Those who spend their Christian lives waiting to be blessed and healed themselves will never go anywhere. The model of Jesus and the model of Paul has to be laid clearly before us, so that we may realise that those who centre upon themselves will at the end of the day live and die for themselves, as irrelevant blips in Church history.

These four steps outlined above, and others like them, inspire Satan's legions as they go forth. From the highest level in the hierarchy of wickedness to the lowest, these plans are being enforced with great zeal and energy. In some nations and churches Satan's strategy is being successful.

In the first centuries A.D., North Africa was one of the most successful church-planting areas of the early Church missionary outreach. The churches were strong and numerous. However, though they had been planted by mission outreach, they quickly forgot how the grace of God had come to them. Engaging themselves in theological debate, they thought themselves to be the defenders of truth, whereas they were at times indifferent to its spread and increase. They largely failed to reach out into other areas of Africa. Perhaps because of that, within a few short centuries they were almost wiped off the map. That region of Africa is now one of the most unreached areas of our generation. Because they did not move out, they have themselves become a mission field once more. As one writer put it, "The church that will not evangelise will fossilise."

If our faith today is not strong enough to cause us to send and be sent in the Name of Christ to the ends of the earth, and to give our all to fight Satan's dark strategies, then we do not have a real faith. The greatest single key to Church growth and success in our day is that we should see the satanic strategy that I have outlined in this chapter for what it is, and then rise up to overcome it, according to the Word of God.

5

Earthen
Vessels

"He chose the lowly things of this world and the despised things – and the things that are not – to nullify the things that are..."   (1 Corinthians 1:28)

Some feel that missionaries are spiritual supermen and superwomen, towering above us on some unreal plane of high spirituality to which we could never attain. When we think of some of the great missionary names over the centuries, from Paul onwards, we tend to see them as a special brand of people. How else could they master different languages and cultures, survive dark jungles and great dangers, and handle the loss of home comforts and loved ones?

Others, as we have seen, regard missionaries as 'religious kamikazes', whose sanity is to be questioned. They may be special, but they are to be ignored as 'peculiar people'.

Whether we see missionaries as special people or peculiar people, the result is the same. We excuse ourselves from world mission, because we see ourselves as 'normal' Christians, but missionaries as 'abnormal' – either above us or below us. We thus conclude that we are unsuitable material for personal involvement in the Great Commission.

In this chapter, I want to look at several great missionary figures from an unusual perspective. The aim is to show that they were ordinary people with ordinary hang-ups – and in some cases even major ones. These hang-ups would be severe enough to disqualify them in many modern contexts. But because they wanted to obey God, because they had a passionate heart to serve Him and reach those without His love, God took them and used them anyway.

They did not wait until they were perfect. They did not wait until they were 'whole'. They simply set out to obey God and His Word. God, because He saw their hearts and their desire to fulfil His call upon their lives, was pleased to bless them – and many others through them.

From these ordinary people we learn a simple lesson. Those who wait for personal blessing and wholeness rarely change anyone, including themselves. They spend their lives waiting for something to happen, caught in a self-centred trap. Those who put the Lord first, others second and themselves third find that God is no man's debtor. He meets them on the road with His love and healing power – to equip them to be yet more effective for Him.

One of the great joys, then, of investigating the records of missionaries over the years is to discover that they were not 'supermen'. They were just ordinary people. It is true that through their labours other races in other nations have turned from darkness to light and found the Saviour. Churches were established, indigenous ministries released. But though their annals speak of these astonishing ways in which God used them, it yet remains equally clear that they were indeed men and women *"just like us"* (James 5:17). In them we recognise ourselves. We see therefore that the glory belongs to God, and not to them. It is their faith in an extraordinary God that marks them out as unusual. They believed that God was powerful enough to use them, 'warts and all'. And He did.

We shall discover that they had certain 'common characteristics' – they were men and women of tremendous devotion to Christ, of prayer, of passion for the Gospel. But there are many dissimilarities between them. They are not clones. In God's Kingdom there is a place for all kinds of people – all those whose hearts are set to obey Him. As we see that, may God speak to us concerning our suitability to join that crowd of witnesses known as 'missionaries'.

Example 1: David Brainerd – the imperfect character[3]

David Brainerd was born in 1718 in Haddam, Connecticut, the

son of a country squire. He was one of nine children who lived with their parents in comfortable circumstances. He was brought up in an environment of New England Puritanism and was affected by the Great Awakening in the United States. He was to become a man of great zeal for God and for His purposes. It has been said that, "Bringing the Gospel to scattered wandering tribes of Indians was his single mission."

But three events in David Brainerd's early life conspired to make him a most unsuitable missionary candidate. They had an effect upon his personality, leaving him less than 'perfect' in his walk with God and with men.

Firstly, his father died when David was eight years old, and his mother when he was only fourteen. These early tragedies, particularly the death of his mother, left a shadow of death over him, and affected his childhood, depriving him of normality and of happiness.

Secondly, given that somewhat morbid disposition, he was further hindered by the influence of an elderly minister, under whom he studied for a few years after the death of his parents. The advice given to him by this teacher was that he should stay away from people of his own age and "cultivate grave, elderly people". Given Brainerd's lack of childhood happiness, that was scarcely suitable advice. Jonathan Edwards, who knew him well, said that although he could be emulated in many ways, his melancholy should not be admired nor imitated.

Thirdly, after enrolling at Yale University at the age of twenty-one in 1739, he was later unjustly expelled. The background to this injustice lay in a move of the Spirit of God in the university, connected with George Whitefield and the Great Awakening. Some of the authorities found this religious enthusiasm unacceptable. They were uneasy with the prayer and Bible study groups which were springing up overnight. In the midst of that, Brainerd made a hostile remark concerning one of his tutors, observing that the tutor had "no more grace" than a chair. The authorities clamped down on Brainerd, using him as a scapegoat. As a result, following his refusal to make a public apology for a private comment, he was expelled. Though attempts were made to have him reinstated, they were never successful.

These three factors, among others, had a deep effect on Brainerd, causing major scars in his life. It was scarcely the ideal preparation for the work of the Lord.

There were also significant flaws in his personality. In November 1742, he responded to a challenge to enlist in missionary work amongst the American Indians with the Society in Scotland for the Propagation of Christian Knowledge in the United States. Following interviews, Brainerd was commissioned to reach out to the Indians in the area of Kaunaumeek, New York. He behaved in a way which seemed once again to render him unsuitable for missionary service. It was planned that he should spend time in language study with John Sergeant, a man who, with his wife, had spent eight years working amongst the Indians, seeing more than one hundred come to Christ and receive baptism. However, Brainerd was too impetuous and independent, and refused to undergo that basic training. Though he was linguistically very unqualified for the work, and lacked suitable training and preparation, he determined to go off by himself into the wilderness to preach to the Indians.

Brainerd's missionary career lasted a mere five years, and he died at the age of twenty-nine as a result of deprivation and the poor conditions in which he lived. Moreover, for more than half of that time he saw little, if any, fruit. He wrote in his diary, "My heart was sunk... it seemed to me I should never have any success amongst the Indians. My soul was weary of my life; I long for death, beyond measure."

However, in the final phase of his short ministry he saw an extraordinary move of the Spirit of God. Relocating in the summer of 1745 to a group of Indians in Crossweeksung in New Jersey, he baptised twenty-five converts within a matter of weeks, and then saw a further deeper visitation of the Spirit of God. Writing concerning August 6th of that year, he said, "Many of them were then much affected and appeared surprisingly tender, so that a few words about their soul's concerns would cause the tears to flow freely, and produce many sobs and groans... Divine truths were attended with a surprising influence and produced a great concern among them. There were scarce three and forty that could refrain from tears and bitter cries."

In the spring of 1746 a church was established, and more revivals followed. However, on a subsequent visit, Brainerd's health broke, and it was clear that he was dying of tuberculosis. His short five year ministry was finished. He died in the home of the great Puritan leader, Jonathan Edwards. He was to have married Jerusha, Jonathan Edwards' daughter, but he died in October 1747; Jerusha died shortly after that.

The effect of Brainerd's life and ministry live on, generations after his death. His diary has remained a classic and a yardstick of genuine spirituality over the years. Significant lives have been changed and inspired by them – men like William Carey and John Wesley, who in their turn have deeply impacted many others.

This short account of Brainerd's career reveals a man in many ways ill-equipped to serve God in such rigorous missionary conditions. I believe that many modern churches would have overlooked him – and perhaps rightly so from some points of view. But they would have missed two elements in his life which, by the grace of God, more than compensated for his scars and failures.

Firstly, Brainerd was a man of tremendous zeal for the Lord and for his missionary calling. Early in his career he wrote, "My work is exceeding hard and difficult; I travel on foot a mile and half, the worst of ways, almost daily, and back; for I live so far from my Indians." Later, when sorely tempted to give up the work, and receiving attractive offers from churches in much more comfortable situations, he resolved, "to go on still with the Indian affair." Like Paul, he was not disobedient to the heavenly vision (Acts 26:19). The passion instilled in him by a desire to obey God's call to the Great Commission carried him through.

Secondly, Brainerd was a man of tremendous prayer. He gave himself to strong prayer, crying out that God's grace might come upon the Indians. God answered his prayer with astonishing power and authority.

God's grace and his own obedience combined for a release of the Holy Spirit on his missionary endeavours that changed the lives of many. Brainerd therefore is a classic example of a man whom God calls and uses. If the key elements of a passion for God's call and a love for the lost are in place, God in His mercy can work around hurts and rebellions that might cause other Brainerds to sideline themselves for a lifetime – or be sidelined by others.

Example 2: William Carey – the man who could 'plod'

William Carey, who was born in 1761 near Northampton, England, served God in the Indian sub-continent. Such was his impact upon mission that he has been described as the 'father of modern missions'. Yet, few men would have seemed less likely to qualify for that honour. Though born to a poor English labouring family, it is said of him that, "More than any other individual in modern history, he stirred the imagination of the Christian world and showed by his own humble example what could and should be done to bring a lost world to Christ."

Carey, like Brainerd, illustrates once more a central truth of mission – that God does not necessarily use unusual people. He uses those who are deeply committed to obey Him. When asked his secret, Carey replied, "I can plod. I can persevere in any definite pursuit. To this, I owe everything."

Carey wanted to be a gardener. But that was not possible because he had allergies. He was apprenticed at the age of sixteen to a shoemaker, an occupation that he pursued until he was twenty- eight. He turned to Christ as a teenager, and God led him to be associated with a group of Baptists, who trained him in the Word of God.

In 1781, he married Dorothy. It was a bad marriage. The more Carey's missionary vision grew, the more his wife struggled. Carey had to embrace this apparently insurmountable blockage to his missionary calling. At the same time, in addition to his responsibility for his own family, he took care of his late master's widow and her four children. In spite of this economic and family pressure, Carey continued faithful to the light God had given him, diligent in his studying and preaching. In 1785, he became pastor of a tiny Baptist church; he then later moved to a larger church at Leicester, though he had to practise his trade to support his family.

At this time Captain Cook's voyages, among other influences, began to open his heart to a wider vision. He therefore sought to develop a biblical perspective on mission. His conclusion was that, "Foreign missions were the central responsibility of the Church." Then, as now, those ideas were seen by others as "irregular" and hardly "mainstream". The general understanding in the eighteenth century was that the Great Commission applied only to the early apostles, and not to the modern Church. A minister with some authority over him responded, "Young man, sit down. When God pleases to convert the heathen, He will do it without your aid or mine." However, Carey persevered, and in 1792 published an 87-page book, *"An Enquiry into the Obligation of Christians to Use Means for the Conversion of the Heathen."* Some say that this ranks as one of the most influential Christian books of all time. Out of that came Carey's motto, "Expect great things from God; attempt great things for God."

In 1792 Carey and others formed the Baptist Missionary Society. There was no substantial financial backing for their work – it demanded tremendous sacrifices from them. Carey immediately offered himself to the new society as a companion to the first missionary. Carey's church was extremely unhappy at his decision, knowing that they would lose their pastor. His father described him as "mad". His wife was strongly opposed – they had three little children and another on the way. Dorothy refused to go. Though distressed by her decision, Carey was equally determined that he would go, even if it meant going alone. On his first trip he set off without her, though the trip had to be aborted. Dorothy then agreed that she would join them, provided that her younger sister, Kitty, could go too.

After arriving in India on June 13th, 1793, Carey faced numerous battles. The influential East India Company was hostile to missionary work because it feared the impact on its profits. They forced the family to move inland, where Dorothy and the two eldest boys became extremely ill. Later their five-year-old son Peter died, an event which caused Dorothy to become "wholly deranged". A colleague commented that Carey often worked "while an insane wife, frequently wrought up to a state of most distressing excitement, was in the next room ..." She died in

1807 at the age of fifty-one[4].

In spite of all the pressures listed above, Carey spent hours every day in Bible translation, as well as preaching and setting up schools. In Serampore, where he laboured for the last thirty-four years of his life, he made three translations of the whole Bible (Bengali, Sanskrit and Marathi). He also helped in other translations of the whole Bible or of the New Testament into many languages and dialects. Even though the quality of the translation was sometimes bad, Carey gave himself to working and reworking it until it could be understood. At the same time, the first twenty-five years of Baptist missions to India saw some six hundred baptised converts, as well as a few thousand more who attended classes and services.

In 1812, Carey lost his massive Polyglot Dictionary, his two grammar books and whole versions of the Bible in a warehouse fire. He accepted that from the Lord and started all over again. Carey founded the Serampore College in 1819 for the training of indigenous church planters and evangelists. He also accepted the position of Professor of Oriental Languages at the Fort William College in Calcutta – an astonishing honour for an uneducated cobbler.

Carey finally died in 1834. He had left his mark upon India and upon missions for all time. His vision – to build indigenous churches "by means of native preachers" and by providing Scriptures in the native language – is one which can be traced backward to Scripture, and forward as the route for future missionary work.

It remains an astonishing fact that an impoverished shoemaker, facing so many trials during his forty-year period of service, could have risen to the stature of one of the great missionaries of all time. Any one of the various factors listed above would have been enough for many folk to feel excused from missionary service – a lack of education, opposition from his local church, a shortage of funds, deficiencies in experience and a difficult marriage. But the fact remains that Carey found God's grace and help to see salvation brought to many, and a model established for missionary endeavour that remains to this day.

Example 3: Gladys Aylward – The London Sparrow

Gladys Aylward applied to join the China Inland Mission, but was rejected in 1931. She was poorly educated and also suffered from a profound learning disability. One biographer comments, "Glady's powers of mental digestion seemed automatically to go into neutral, and occasionally reverse." Yet this diminutive London lass, born into a working-class family in 1902, became one of the most celebrated single women missionaries in modern history.

Gladys Aylward went to work at the age of fourteen as a parlour-maid, performing routine tasks by day, and subject to curfew by night. Most of her excitement in those days came from her dreams – of drinking, smoking, dancing, gambling and theatres! But after she had turned to Christ in her twenties, she quickly surrendered her life to serve the Lord in mission. She took every opportunity to learn about China. Lacking any other means to go, she determined to go alone. Having saved hard, she bought a railway ticket to travel to China through Europe, Russia and Siberia. On October 15th 1932, she set out for China from London's Liverpool Street Station, intending to work with a widowed missionary. Astonishingly she was kept safe while crossing Russia at a time when there was an undeclared border war between Russia and China. By God's grace alone she passed through the war front, where no one except military folk were expected to travel, and arrived safely in China.

After falling out with the missionary whom she had gone out to help, Gladys was asked by the Chinese magistrate Yang Cheng to become the local foot inspector, a task related to the new laws against female foot-binding. It was an ideal opportunity to enter Chinese homes, and Gladys embraced it. She travelled from village to village making many friends and converts.

However, in 1937, as the instability in China brought changes and dangers, she had to move on. There followed a period involving her famous work with orphans, and the astonishing journey with nearly one hundred children in 1940 across the mountains and the Yellow River to safety from the Japanese invaders.

The latter period of Gladys' life, after the mainland had closed to missionary work, saw her travelling widely, based in Taiwan – she had taken Chinese citizenship. A popular biography, "The Small Woman" by Alan Burgess, was written. The film, "The Inn of the Sixth Happiness" was made, based on that book. She spoke in Hollywood's First Presbyterian Church. She appeared on BBC television. She also dined with the Queen and received many other honours.

She said that her secret was a simple one, "I wasn't God's first choice for what I have done for China. There was somebody else... I do not know who it was – God's first choice. It must have been a man – a wonderful man. A well-educated man. I don't know what happened. Perhaps he died. Perhaps he wasn't willing... and God looked down... and saw Gladys Aylward." She clearly saw herself as a substitute for someone more highly qualified.

But the required passions were there – a passion for God, a passion for His call to missions, a passion for the impossible. And thus a single woman, small in stature but great in faith, overcame personal loneliness, difficulties in learning, battles with fellow workers and other obstacles, and brought life in Christ Jesus to many, many lives.

Once more I am forced to conclude that many modern churches would have tried to keep Gladys Aylward in her place, seeing her as unqualified in education and spiritual disposition for this work. But she reckoned otherwise – and so did God. The rest is history.

Example 4: John Sung – the fiery scholar-preacher

John Sung (Song Shangjie) was born in China in September, 1901 and died in August, 1944, shortly before his 43rd birthday. Yet in that short lifetime God used him to make a dramatic impact for revival in China and in other Asian lands.

Sung's temperament was in some ways far from ideal. He is reported as saying that the Lord had to curtail his life span because of his ungracious attitude to others, including foreign missionaries. Descriptions of him such as 'rude', 'abrupt', 'stubborn', 'unprepossessing' would not be out of place. But God saw the heart, and still used him – and many found Christ because of that.

He was born the sixth child of a Chinese pastor. His father dedicated him to God while he was in the womb, because he was the first child born to them after his mother's conversion. He grew up in relative poverty, a fact not altogether surprising since the Sung family finished with ten children!

When he was nine, revival came to Sung's village and he was saved. He was fascinated by Bible stories and showed great aptitude for learning. But he was a child of action as well as study. During his school holidays he organised evangelistic bands with his school friends, travelling to nearby villages to proclaim the Gospel and hold Bible classes.

However, when he later went to study in the United States, his academic interests overshadowed his Christian commitment. His love for the Lord grew cold and stale. But the Lord met him there with unusual grace. Various events in Sung's life at that time produced such inner conflicts in him that his college principal sent him to a mental institution to undergo several weeks of psychiatric evaluation. There Sung rediscovered his love for God and His Word. He gave much time in that unlikely place to reading the Bible.

The Lord made it clear to him that he was to return to China for the work of evangelism. On his return, he said to his father, "I have dedicated my life to the preaching of the Gospel." He turned down a very lucrative job with the government in order to do this. Sung spent the rest of his life in fearless and tireless service for the Lord. He preached the Gospel, set up Bible Institutes, organised preaching bands, travelling widely and preaching at every opportunity in order to win souls for Jesus. God honoured his work. He saw moves of God throughout China. After one such revival, Sung commented, "There are three secrets of revival: one, a thorough confession of sin; two, prayer for the fullness of the Holy Spirit; three, public witness for Christ." That basic and direct apostolic Christianity, which he himself lived by, changed lives and even communities in China, Taiwan, the Philippines, Indonesia and other nations to which he journeyed.

One who knew him said after his death, "Thank God for Dr. Sung. He must be one of the happiest men in Heaven because he has led many souls, and those souls went to Heaven continually. They thank God and they thank Dr. Sung..." John Sung is not 'lonely in heaven' – to borrow Oswald J. Smith's parable again. Sung gave himself to taking the Gospel to those who had not heard, and to inspiring others to do so. 'John Chinaman' will indeed seek him out!

Today there are countless other examples of the kind of people that God uses as missionaries. Their testimonies are just as thrilling as those in this chapter. John Sung stands as a forerunner of an astonishing move of God. Today's missionary task force is no longer exclusively white and Western. Some estimate that by AD 2000 there will be more non-western missionaries than Western ones. Lands like Korea, India, Nigeria, Brazil and Indonesia are at the front of these thrilling events.

Wherever they come from, two great strands will continue to manifest in them. Firstly, they are ordinary men and women like you and me. They have personal failings; they have areas that have not yet been dealt with at the Cross. At times they know defeat and discouragement. They are capable of battles with their fellow workers, which sometimes lead to division and hostility. They are sometimes ill-equipped to a degree that could be called serious, both in their spiritual and educational background. They are far from perfect.

But, secondly, they know the grace of God in His calling and empowering. They have responded to His call and made themselves available, often with great sacrifice, for Him to use in this critical matter of world mission. They simply offer themselves to be vessels of His love for the lost in all the nations on earth. They have allowed His heart of compassion to overwhelm their own cold hearts.

Maybe there is a Gladys Aylward reading these pages, someone whose heart God has already stirred. Perhaps there is a John Sung, lost in theory and in his books, whose heart needs to be lit by the flame of God's fire for the lost. Perhaps there is a Brainerd, morose with the pain of injustice and loss, whose heart can yet be an altar for a call of God that will change many lives. Perhaps there is some Asian, South American or African William Carey, born in some hidden place and yet with the call of God to prominence in world mission upon his life.

> *"Think of what you were when you were called. Not many of you were wise by human standards; not many were influential; not many were of noble birth. But God chose the foolish things of the world to shame the wise; God chose the weak things of the world to shame the strong. He chose the lowly things of this world and the despised things – and the things that are not – to nullify the things that are..."*
>
> *(1 Corinthians 1:26-28)*

God has consistently chosen "foolish" people, "weak" people, "lowly" people to do His purposes. He looks for them again today.

---

[3]Material from this chapter has been taken from the highly recommended book of missionary biographies entitled **"From Jerusalem to Irian Jaya"** by Ruth A. Tucker (Zondervan).
[4]It is not easy to understand these events. Carey later remarried very happily.

6

Five Steps to
Change the World

"In the church at Antioch there were prophets and teachers... While they were worshipping the Lord and fasting, the Holy Spirit said, 'Set apart for me Barnabas and Saul for the work to which I have called them.' So after they had fasted and prayed, they placed their hands on them and sent them off." (Acts 13:1-3)

If mission is the central responsibility of the Church, there must be specific steps and a defined route down which we can travel towards that goal. The purpose of this chapter is to describe five steps along that path.

Step 1: Embrace Mission

Many Christians today come from a background that makes them relatively ignorant and untaught on the subject of mission. They will have to open their hearts and minds to understand it. They will have to embrace nations, peoples and groups who are quite different from them. They will have to learn about God's purposes for these peoples so that they begin to love them.

Since vision and burden are born out of exposure to need, there must be regular, disciplined teaching on mission. It is not easy for us to understand and identify with other cultures and peoples. There must therefore be regular missionary weekends. Missionaries (some of whom may not fit neat church patterns) must be invited to share their hearts. Certainly there are problems here, as not all missionaries make good speakers. But where there is a heart, there is a way.

Firstly, **identify** the country or people group that God is calling us to serve. Secondly, **find out** about them[5]. When we read newspapers and magazines, we need to look for relevant news items. That may necessitate changing our newspaper, and reading books and magazines which we might not otherwise read. In a word, we need to share God's heart for a people to whom we would not naturally relate. Embracing mission is an act of the will and of the mind, a deliberate decision.

Step 2: Pray for Mission

The logical extension of embracing God's heart for another people or nation is that we should pray for them. Having obtained information and understanding, we then carry that information to the Throne of Grace in prayer. We need to make prayer for mission a priority.

The apostle John says, *"This is the confidence we have in approaching God: that if we ask anything according to His will, He hears us. And if we know that He hears us – whatever we ask – we know that we have what we asked of Him"* (1 John 5:14-15). When a Christian is convinced that mission is in accordance with the will of God, he then will have great liberty and authority in prayer for it.

We must pray specifically for the nations and peoples and missionaries that God has laid on our hearts. From the Scriptures and from the Holy Spirit we can define God's will for the people we are praying for. That will include the winning of men and women to Christ; the nurturing and upbuilding of the new converts and churches in the Word of God; and the training of indigenous leadership.

This kind of prayer must take priority, even a tithe of our prayer-time. We will be pulled away from prayer for mission. So we must constantly be on our guard against that both in private and corporate times of prayer. That will take discipline. There is also a need to seek out others who will form a missions prayer group – for China, India or any other nation which God has called us to adopt. Such groups need to meet sacrificially and regularly, with one person within them responsible for obtaining related information[6]. Missionary workers must also be identified and prayed for in that way. Church leadership must take a lead in such prayer. Every part of the church's prayer-life, from the individual and secret time to the open and corporate time, should be richly permeated by prayer for world mission.

Step 3: Give to Missions

The next logical progression will be in the area of church giving. We cannot pray effectively unless we are willing ourselves to be a part of the answer. One important aspect of that answer will be generous giving to the work of missions. Peter Marshall laid a challenge before us when he said, "Give according to your income, lest God make your income according to your giving." That applies to both churches and individuals. There are remarkable testimonies of pastors who have set out to put mission first. One reached and sustained a target of over fifty percent of church income being given to mission.

Often, however, giving to mission is the last area considered by a church. When pastors, assistant pastors, youth workers, worship leaders and caretakers have been paid, when the building project has reached its monthly target, then the struggling missionaries and missionary societies are considered. We need to reverse that. We must set deliberate, specific and bold missionary budgets, and then give the rest to the local needs. It is unacceptable before God that local leaders should control church finances for their own purposes. The finances do not belong to them. They belong to the Lord of the harvest-field.

Step 4: Go – send and be sent

In Luke 10:1-3 Jesus gave very clear instructions to His disciples: *"After this the Lord appointed seventy-two others and sent them two by two ahead of Him to every town and place where He was about to go. He told them, 'The harvest is plentiful, but the workers are few. Ask the Lord of the harvest, therefore, to send out workers into His harvest field. Go! I am sending you out like lambs among wolves.'"* The clear pattern that Jesus reveals here is that prayer logically leads to going; and that going then leads to more prayer that others might go again.

In all that we do, our objective must be to see Christians go from local churches into all the world. It is God's heart to see His people **go**. David Brainerd went; Gladys Aylward went; John Sung and William Carey went. The bottom-line of Church activity is that folk should go.

Acts 13:1-3 gives a model to be emulated by every church. The passage describes how Paul and Barnabas were released and sent out from the new and fast-growing work in Antioch. The church in Antioch did not select their problem people to go to the ends of earth. They released the best. Paul and Barnabas were genuine apostles, much needed in the local church. Some pastors and churches are willing for the dispensable people in their churches to go, but not those they feel are essential to their local work. That is understandable, because in many cases they have spent much time preparing them for the work of the ministry. But the Lord Himself claims the Church and all in it for His own greatest purposes. The best must be released to go.

They might be released in the traditional way to a missionary society, or directly to serve under indigenous leadership in some growing overseas church, or to a missionary outreach of the sending church. God will make a way, when we release those that He has chosen – especially the best that we have.

For that to happen, churches must establish a specific 'going programme'. This sending schedule must include at least five elements:

A. A short-term missions programme.

In this day and age, with reasonably affordable and speedy air flights to and from most countries, young and older people alike can be encouraged to go on mission trips that last from a few days to a few months[7]. For example, in China there are at least five kinds of possible short-term mission teams – intercession teams, low-key evangelism teams, leadership training teams, courier teams (carrying in Christian literature) and teams working in children's homes. Each country has these or other similar possibilities.

B. Outreach ventures by the local church.
Involvement by churches in specific ventures to other countries provides a means for church members to see mission at first hand. Joint ventures to serve local churches in accessible countries can be helpful both to those who go and those who receive them. Teams can potentially go out several times a year. However, churches must be disciplined in their planning for these events. Church leaders must not allow these ventures to start but not to finish. Christians must be taught to prioritise mission activity, and not to allow it to slip into oblivion through ill-attention from leadership. Equally, the sending teams must have a heart to serve and not to lord it over the churches in the countries that receive them.

C. A vision for tentmakers.
Businessmen, teachers and other professionals, as well as students, with a capacity to work or study abroad should be encouraged to do so. Whether for longer or for shorter periods, this rich resource of those who can walk in the footsteps of the apostle Paul should be released and assisted.

D. A long-term missionary-sending strategy.
There must be specific objectives to send those who will go out for longer periods – two missionaries after five years, ten after ten years and so on. This will include practical and irreversible determination to send and to support the missionaries who go out. Short-term ventures are helpful, but they must not be allowed to replace lifetime commitments.

E. Leadership visits to the field.
Local church leaders should visit the field regularly. This is not in order to expand their own ministries, in terms of preaching opportunities, but to submit themselves to a wider world view. They should also on these visits serve those who have gone out from their churches to the mission field by listening to and

encouraging them. It is strategic that leaders be servants here, not masters. It is vital that they share the heart of God for the vast areas of the world beyond their own localities.

Acts 13 again gives a powerful challenge in this whole area. Antioch was a successful church. It was headed by Paul and Barnabas. It was growing fast. The believers were first recognised as distinct and given the name 'Christians' there. They were financially strong enough to help the church in Jerusalem because of their own abundance. But the response of some leaders in Antioch (Acts 13:1) was to wait on the Lord to see why He had blessed them so richly. As they did that, God gave them His answer. It was so that they might send out Paul and Barnabas to the work for which He had called them – the work of missions.

If they had not waited on Him, in all their abundance and their success, they might have missed the purposes of God in their generation. They might have built a large and successful church, but have resisted God's plan to extend way beyond their limited borders. May God help us not to do that in our generation.

Step 5: Support Missionaries

Having gone out, missionaries can often be lonely and isolated. When they first set out, leaving the local church behind, there is a warmth towards them in the hearts of the people. But after a short period they tend to be forgotten. Letters and phone calls dry up. Church events in their home countries take place without their being informed. They are more and more out on a limb, forgotten and seemingly irrelevant.

It is vital that some within the churches form support groups for those who have gone out so that this chasm of isolation is bridged. When others cease to care, the support groups will remember to love those who have gone out at a great price. They will not forget birthdays and anniversaries. They will keep in touch about church and local news. They will send books, food and gifts – just to show that they still care. One pastor's wife I know addresses and dates airmail letters to the missionaries. She then hands them out on Sunday mornings to the Christians in her church. In this way she ensures the local Christians have specific dates on which they must write to those on the mission field.

The aim of support groups is a simple one. It is to make sure the missionaries know they are not forgotten, but that they are loved and appreciated, even though they are far away from the local church.

The five steps outlined above might at first sight seem costly. But they are attainable. They require regular reviews of all church programmes and teaching, finances, and general spheres of interest. Again and again, the church leaders must look to see whether they are encouraging the people to be believers in mission – or fostering unbelief through their own neglect of the Great Commission.

My mind goes back again to Acts 13, to that small group of believers seeking the face of God in Antioch. They heard God and they took a costly step. How could they know at the time that their sacrificial release of Paul and Barnabas would change the lives of possibly millions of people, and set in motion a river of grace that still flows today. Yes, these five steps are costly – but they also contain within them the elements to release new 'Pauls', and through them new grace from God into the lives of thousands who are still waiting to hear the Gospel. May God help us to take specific steps along this path in obedience to His commands.

[5]Patrick Johnstone's book **"Operation World"** (OM Publishing) is an invaluable tool in this process. It also includes addresses of missionary organisations which you can contact.
[6]Missionary societies and individual missionaries will be delighted to supply prayer material for such purposes.
[7]Many sending groups can advise on ways to do this.

7

Let's Do It

"I was not disobedient to the heavenly vision." (Acts 26:19)

We can respond in various ways to the challenge of world mission that this book brings. Some responses are manifestly wrong and unacceptable – negative reactions of outright rejection or rank indifference. However, there is one which is more subtle, and therefore more dangerous, because it is unseen. This reaction I will call "assent", as opposed to the necessary response of "belief".

Irrespective of other uses, the word "assent" here is taken to mean that state of mind which accepts everything that is said intellectually, but which does not do anything about it practically. The most impassioned pleas for obedience to the Great Commission can be heard, agreed with – but yet ignored.

"Belief", as defined here, is that state of mind and spirit which hears the commands of Scripture, receives them and seeks to bear fruit. That fruit will be seen in various ways, some of which have been defined in this book. These include embracing mission; praying for nations and for missionaries; giving to mission as a priority; supporting those who go; and, most of all, sending and being sent on mission to the nations.

Significantly, when Jesus taught the parable of the sower (Mark 4:1-20), He stressed that the seed sown into good soil will *"hear the word, accept it, and produce a crop – thirty, sixty or even a hundred times what was sown"* (Mark 4:20). That is a very clear definition of what it means to "believe". It is clearly more than simply "assenting". It also involves producing a crop.

In other words, where God's Word is heard and believed, there is measurable change and definable product brought into the life of the one who hears it, and into the lives of others through him. That truth applies pre-eminently to mission. It is not enough to agree. There must be visible change and commitment in our lives.

One of the great dangers in the modern Church is that leaders and Christians accept the teaching on mission, but they do not believe it. Pastors will stand at the front of churches and teach the people about mission. They will speak in terms of "you need to learn..." But when the fruit-bearing areas of the lives of these pastors and believers are measured, there is no "mission-fruit". There is but little prayer for missions, and less giving. Few are encouraged to go out on mission trips, especially for lifetime commitments.

In fact, there may be an active culture within the Church working against "praying, giving and going" for mission. Some leaders are threatened by the thought that their people or finances or prayer power might be given to something which will not be measurable within the local church. The danger then is that we "assent", but have no desire to "believe".

Paul stands as a great model in this matter. If we wish to know whether we "assent" or "believe" (as defined above), then we can freely measure ourselves by Paul's example. In Acts 16, Paul was working in the region of Phrygia and Galatia (v6). It is clear that he wished to reach in to other regions with the Gospel. The missionary burden was strong upon him. The Holy Spirit refused him permission to go into Asia and then into Bithynia (vv 6-7). However, in Troas Paul receives a vision of a man from Macedonia, begging him to come over and help them (v9). Paul's response to that (v10) is a classic missionary one – he immediately prepared to leave for Macedonia, concluding that God had called him to preach the Gospel there.

There is within that the very clear understanding that Paul was available to God to travel for the Gospel's sake. Whatever "goldmine" he may have been sitting on in Troas paled into insignificance in comparison with a man and a people crying out for the opportunity to hear the Gospel.

In verses 11-15 Paul arrived in Philippi, the leading city of that district of Macedonia. Significantly, it was a Roman colony, and probably did not have a synagogue. Therefore, on the Sabbath Paul went out to find a place of prayer – outside the city. There he encountered a group of spiritually-inclined, but as yet unconverted, women at prayer. He preached Jesus to them, and God's grace was there for Lydia and others to turn to Christ.

Following baptism, Lydia, an influential businesswoman, invited Paul and his party to stay in her home. It was a classic pastoral situation. A Christian group had been formed, of which Paul was the clearly recognised pastor. Those who had turned to Christ under his ministry were deeply grateful and therefore intensely warm towards him, and wished to provide comfortable accommodation and possibly financial support for the ministry. The obvious response was for Paul to settle down there for a season and build that group into a fully functioning church. But Paul's heart was set on penetrating into the city.

There then began in verse sixteen a most extraordinary series of events. Paul was confronted by a demon-possessed slave-girl with an occult fortune-telling ability. Her clairvoyant powers were exploited by businessmen to make money. The spirits were so confident of their dark hold upon the city of Philippi that they did not fear to give free advertising to Paul (*"These men are servants of the Most High God, who are telling you the way to be saved."* v17). They believed that he could not establish a Christian group inside the city. But Paul pressed in – driving the evil spirits out of the girl, facing the rage of those who had hoped to make more money out of her, and then braving the injustice of the authorities in the market place. Paul and Silas were arrested, then severely and unjustly punished. They were stripped and flogged, and thrown untended into prison.

The astonishing truth here is that Paul had no need to endure that. In verses 35-40 it is subsequently revealed that Paul, as a Roman citizen, should not have been subject to such punishment. Roman citizens were protected by law from this kind of rough justice. Later, when they knew what they had done to Paul, the magistrates themselves were clearly terrified (vv 38-39), because Paul, as a Roman citizen, could have had them arrested for their treatment of him.

Why did Paul endure that severe flogging when he knew that he could avoid it by merely declaring his Roman citizenship? Much as I have considered this question, I can only come up with one answer. I believe Paul had a strong conviction that in this particular situation he had to endure it for the sake of the Gospel, and therefore he remained silent under it.

The results of that are clear. While Paul and Silas were in prison overnight, God visited the prison, and the jailer and his household were saved. There, in the heart of the prison, God planted the church in Philippi. In God's providence, Paul's missionary calling took him inside the prison to reach the jailer.

Acts 16 shows the commitment and courage of the apostle Paul in the face of awful suffering. He had fully embraced the promises and commands of the Lord Jesus – to go into all the world (including the prison cells) with the Gospel, because he believed Jesus would be with him even in that place. The end result was that another city was opened to God's love and a church was planted. The letter to the Philippians that he later wrote is one of the most encouraging and joy-filled in all of Scripture. This church obviously grew and prospered.

None of us wants to be flogged, even for Jesus! But God can be trusted not to take us beyond what we can endure – and to offer the great joy, more powerful than any pain that we might face, of seeing men and women find the eternal love of the Lord Jesus Christ. Surely our brief pains and pressures fade into insignificance in that light!

Those who merely **assent** will settle outside the city with the "Lydias". There is nothing wrong with that in itself – the grace of God is clearly there for "Lydias" as well as for others. But the hard fact of the matter is that the jailer and others inside the city will remain unsaved if we do not press in to wherever **belief** may take us.

Although the example is exceptional, the challenge is real. Those who **believe** in the Gospel message will be prepared to pay a price in whatever ways God leads them. They will give of themselves and of their substance. They will pray and they will go. They will embrace and they will support... for the Gospel's sake.

The intent of this small book is simple. The information contained in it is sufficient to inform us concerning the Great Commission – the one overruling task of the Church world-wide in every age. What the book cannot supply is our decision. Are we prepared to move from ignorance or 'assent' into belief? Are we prepared, as the Father has done Himself, to give sacrificially for missions? *"God had an only Son, and He made Him a missionary."* If it was good enough for the Creator of the universe, it must be good enough for the Church in our generation – for you and for me.

There are challenges like Philippi that face us in our world today. Luis Bush, speaking at the 1989 Lausanne Conference in Manila, referred to the number of peoples unreached with the Gospel who "live in a belt that extends from West Africa across Asia, between ten degrees North to forty degrees North of the Equator. This includes the Muslim block, the Hindu block, and the Buddhist block..." The peoples of this block, which has come to be known as the 10/40 Window, will not hear the Good News of Jesus in their own languages, nor see an increase of indigenous churches, if we do not give to them in our day what Paul gave to Philippi in his day. We can settle for the Lydias outside the city. Or we can obey Christ, and penetrate these strongholds, as Paul did long ago.

Then, and only then, will we see multitudes from the 10/40 window, and from all the peoples of the earth, standing with us before the throne of grace, singing *"a new song: 'You are worthy to take the scroll and to open its seals, because You were slain, and with Your blood You purchased men for God from every tribe and language and people and nation.'"* (Revelation 5:9).

Other books by Ross Paterson, published by Sovereign World:

Heartcry for China (1989)
China: The Hidden Miracle (1993)

For specifics on where to pray for and where to go, we highly recommend the following two books: *Operation World* by Patrick Johnstone (OM Publishing) and *Nine Worlds to Win* by Floyd McClung Jr. and Kalafi Moala (Word).

Publisher's Postscript:

If you have been challenged by this book, as I have been, please write to me at the following address and I will forward your letter to an appropriate missionary society or to Ross Paterson the author.

Chris Mungeam
Sovereign World Limited
P.O. Box 777
Tonbridge
Kent, TN11 9XT,
England.